Business Law for the Modern Entrepreneur: Building a Strong Legal Foundation for Your Business

Frederic BEHE

Chapter 1: Introduction to Legal and Regulatory Considerations

Chapter 1 provides an overview of the legal and regulatory landscape that entrepreneurs face when starting and running a business. Entrepreneurs must navigate a complex web of laws and regulations that govern their activities, including intellectual property law, employment law, and tax law, among others.

This chapter introduces the importance of legal and regulatory compliance for entrepreneurs and the potential consequences of noncompliance. We will explore the key legal and regulatory considerations that entrepreneurs must understand and address to operate a successful and sustainable business.
In addition, this chapter will provide an overview of intellectual property law, employment law, and tax law, which are among the most critical areas of law for entrepreneurs. By understanding the basic concepts and principles of these areas of law, entrepreneurs can effectively manage legal risks and protect their businesses.

This chapter sets the foundation for the rest of the book by highlighting the critical role of legal and regulatory considerations in the success of an entrepreneurial venture.

1.1 Understanding the Importance of Legal and Regulatory Compliance

Legal and regulatory compliance is crucial for any business, especially for entrepreneurs. Failure to comply with applicable laws and regulations can result in serious legal and financial consequences that can derail a business, damage its reputation, and even lead to criminal charges.

Compliance means conforming to legal and regulatory requirements, and it involves much more than just obeying the law. Compliance also involves implementing policies and procedures to ensure that a business is operating in an ethical and socially responsible manner, protecting the interests of stakeholders, and mitigating risks.

For entrepreneurs, compliance is particularly important because they often lack the resources and experience to navigate complex legal and regulatory requirements. Startups and small businesses are at risk of noncompliance due to a lack of awareness, inadequate resources, or poor planning.

Entrepreneurs may be tempted to cut corners or take shortcuts to save money or time, especially in the early stages of their venture. However, noncompliance can be costly, both financially and reputationally. For instance, a startup that violates intellectual property rights or employment laws may face lawsuits, fines, or damage to its brand and reputation.

On the other hand, compliance can be a competitive advantage for businesses. Compliance can demonstrate to investors, customers, and other stakeholders that a business is trustworthy, ethical, and committed to best practices. Compliance can also help businesses avoid costly legal disputes and regulatory enforcement actions.

Compliance is a critical aspect of operating a successful and sustainable business. Entrepreneurs must understand the importance of legal and regulatory compliance and take proactive steps to ensure that their business is compliant with applicable laws and regulations. This includes implementing compliance policies and procedures, training employees, and seeking expert advice when necessary.

1.2 Overview of Intellectual Property Law

Intellectual property (IP) law is a critical area of law for entrepreneurs, as it protects the intangible assets of a business, such as inventions, trademarks, copyrights, and trade secrets. IP law provides entrepreneurs with the legal tools to monetize their ideas and innovations, gain a competitive advantage, and build a strong brand.

IP law can be divided into several categories, including patent law, trademark law, copyright law, and trade secret law. Each of these categories provides different types of legal protection for different types of intangible assets.

Patent law protects new and useful inventions, processes, machines, and compositions of matter. Patents give inventors the exclusive right to make, use, and sell their invention for a limited time, usually 20 years from the date of filing.

Trademark law protects brand names, logos, and other distinctive marks that identify a business's products or services. Trademarks can be registered with the U.S. Patent and Trademark Office (USPTO) to provide nationwide protection against infringement.

Copyright law protects original works of authorship, such as literary, artistic, and musical works, as well as software and digital content. Copyright owners have the exclusive right to reproduce, distribute, and display their works, and can sue infringers for damages and injunctive relief.

Trade secret law protects confidential business information, such as formulas, processes, and customer lists, that give a business a competitive advantage. Trade secret owners must take reasonable steps to keep their information confidential, and can sue for damages and injunctive relief if their trade secrets are misappropriated.

IP law also includes licensing agreements, technology transfers, and other legal mechanisms for monetizing and protecting intangible assets.

Entrepreneurs must understand the basics of IP law and take proactive steps to protect their intellectual property. This includes conducting IP searches, filing patent and trademark applications, and implementing policies and procedures to protect trade secrets and confidential information. By doing so, entrepreneurs can safeguard their innovations and assets and maximize their value and impact.

1.3 Overview of Employment Law

Employment law is a critical area of law for entrepreneurs, as it governs the relationship between employers and employees. Employment law includes a wide range of legal requirements, such as anti-discrimination laws, wage and hour laws, and health and safety regulations. Compliance with employment law is essential for entrepreneurs to avoid costly legal disputes and reputational damage.

Anti-discrimination laws prohibit employers from discriminating against employees or job applicants based on their protected characteristics, such as race, gender, age, or disability. Employers must ensure that their employment practices, including hiring, firing, promotions, and compensation, are fair and non-discriminatory.

Wage and hour laws regulate minimum wage, overtime pay, and other terms and conditions of employment. Employers must comply with these laws, which can vary by state and industry, to avoid wage and hour disputes and legal liability.

Health and safety regulations require employers to provide a safe and healthy workplace for their employees. Employers must comply with OSHA regulations, which mandate safety standards for various industries and impose penalties for noncompliance.

Employment law also covers other aspects of the employer-employee relationship, such as employee benefits, leave policies, and termination procedures. Employers must ensure that their policies and procedures comply with applicable employment laws and regulations to avoid legal disputes and reputational damage.

Entrepreneurs must understand the basics of employment law and take proactive steps to comply with legal requirements. This includes developing employment policies and procedures, training employees and managers, and seeking expert advice when necessary. By doing so, entrepreneurs can create a positive and productive workplace and avoid costly legal disputes and reputational damage.

1.4 Overview of Tax Law

Tax law is a critical area of law for entrepreneurs, as it governs the taxation of businesses and individuals. Tax law includes federal, state, and local taxes, and compliance with tax laws is essential for entrepreneurs to avoid penalties and legal liability.

Tax law covers various types of taxes, including income taxes, sales taxes, property taxes, and payroll taxes. Entrepreneurs must understand the tax laws applicable to their business and comply with them to avoid legal disputes and penalties.

Income taxes are taxes on a business's net income, which is calculated by subtracting its expenses from its revenue. Entrepreneurs must file federal and state income tax returns and pay taxes on their business's net income. The tax laws applicable to small businesses can be complex, and entrepreneurs may need to seek expert advice to ensure compliance.

Sales taxes are taxes on the sale of goods and services, and the rules governing sales taxes can vary by state and industry. Entrepreneurs must collect and remit sales taxes to the appropriate authorities and comply with various sales tax laws and regulations.

Property taxes are taxes on real estate and other tangible property, and the rules governing property taxes can vary by state and locality. Entrepreneurs must pay property taxes on their business's real estate and other property and comply with various property tax laws and regulations.

Payroll taxes are taxes on employee wages and salaries, and employers must withhold and remit these taxes to the appropriate authorities. Employers must comply with various payroll tax laws and regulations, such as those governing Social Security and Medicare taxes.

Entrepreneurs must understand the basics of tax law and take proactive steps to comply with legal requirements. This includes keeping accurate records, filing tax returns on time, and seeking expert advice when necessary. By doing so, entrepreneurs can avoid legal disputes and penalties and ensure that their business operations are financially sound.

Chapter 2: Intellectual Property Law

Chapter 2 provides an overview of intellectual property law, which is a critical area of law for entrepreneurs. Intellectual property law governs the protection and use of creative and innovative works, including inventions, trademarks, copyrights, and trade secrets. Understanding intellectual property law is essential for entrepreneurs to protect their valuable intellectual property assets, avoid legal disputes, and capitalize on their innovations and creativity.

This chapter will explore the basics of intellectual property law, including the different types of intellectual property, how to obtain and enforce intellectual property rights, and the challenges and opportunities of intellectual property law for entrepreneurs. It will also cover the international aspects of intellectual property law and the emerging issues in the field, such as the impact of technology and the rise of open source and collaborative innovation.

By the end of this chapter, entrepreneurs will have a solid understanding of the fundamentals of intellectual property law and how to navigate this complex area of law to protect and leverage their intellectual property assets.

2.1 Patents and Trade Secrets

Patents and trade secrets are two of the most important types of intellectual property protection for entrepreneurs. Patents are legal protections granted by the government that give inventors the exclusive right to use, manufacture, and sell their inventions for a set period, typically 20 years from the date of filing. Trade secrets, on the other hand, are confidential information, such as formulas, processes, and techniques, that give a business a competitive advantage and are not generally known to the public.

Patents are particularly important for entrepreneurs who develop new products, processes, or technologies. By obtaining a patent, an entrepreneur can prevent others from using, making, or selling their invention without permission. To obtain a patent, an entrepreneur must file a patent application with the U.S. Patent and Trademark Office (USPTO) and meet certain legal requirements, such as demonstrating that the invention is novel, non-obvious, and useful. The patent application process can be complex and time-consuming, but it is essential for protecting valuable inventions and securing a competitive advantage.

Trade secrets, on the other hand, are particularly important for entrepreneurs who have confidential information that is not patentable, such as customer lists, marketing strategies, and manufacturing processes. Trade secrets can provide a competitive advantage by giving a business unique insights or methods that are not available to competitors. To protect trade secrets, entrepreneurs must take reasonable steps to keep the information confidential, such as using non-disclosure agreements, restricting access to the information, and implementing security measures.

Patents and trade secrets are not mutually exclusive, and entrepreneurs may use both types of protection for different aspects of their intellectual property. For example, an entrepreneur may file a patent application to protect a new product or process, while also using trade secret protection to keep the details of their manufacturing process confidential.

Patents and trade secrets are critical tools for entrepreneurs to protect their valuable intellectual property assets and gain a competitive advantage in the marketplace. By understanding the basics of patent and trade secret law, entrepreneurs can take proactive steps to protect their intellectual property and avoid legal disputes.

2.2 Copyright Law

Copyright law is a branch of intellectual property law that protects creative works, such as books, music, movies, and software. Copyright protection gives the author or creator of a work the exclusive right to control how the work is used, reproduced, and distributed. Copyright protection is automatic and applies to any original work of authorship that is fixed in a tangible medium, such as a written document or a digital file.

For entrepreneurs, copyright law is particularly important for protecting their creative works, such as marketing materials, website content, and software code. By obtaining copyright protection, entrepreneurs can prevent others from using their works without permission and can pursue legal action against those who infringe on their rights.

To obtain copyright protection, an entrepreneur does not need to file any formal application with the government. However, registering a copyright with the U.S. Copyright Office provides certain benefits, such as the ability to sue for infringement and recover statutory damages. The copyright registration process is relatively simple and can be completed online.

One challenge for entrepreneurs is navigating the complex rules and exceptions in copyright law. For example, the "fair use" doctrine allows for limited use of copyrighted works for purposes such as criticism, comment, news reporting, teaching, scholarship, or research. It can be difficult for entrepreneurs to determine whether their use of a copyrighted work falls within the bounds of fair use or constitutes infringement.

Another challenge is the international nature of copyright law. Copyright protection varies from country to country, and entrepreneurs doing business internationally must understand the legal requirements in each jurisdiction.

Overall, copyright law is a critical area of law for entrepreneurs, as it protects their valuable creative works and gives them a competitive advantage in the marketplace. By understanding the basics of copyright law and working with legal professionals, entrepreneurs can ensure that their works are protected and avoid legal disputes related to infringement.

2.3 Trademark Law

Trademark law is a branch of intellectual property law that protects names, logos, slogans, and other identifying marks used in commerce to distinguish one business from another. Trademarks give entrepreneurs the exclusive right to use their marks in connection with the sale of goods or services and prevent others from using similar marks that may confuse consumers.

For entrepreneurs, trademarks are critical for building brand recognition and establishing a reputation in the marketplace. A strong trademark can be a valuable asset, as it can increase consumer confidence and loyalty, and differentiate a business from competitors.

To obtain trademark protection, an entrepreneur must file a trademark application with the U.S. Patent and Trademark Office (USPTO) and meet certain legal requirements, such as demonstrating that the mark is distinctive and not likely to cause confusion with existing marks. The trademark registration process can be complex and time-consuming, but it is essential for protecting valuable marks and securing a competitive advantage.

One challenge for entrepreneurs is ensuring that their trademark is not infringing on the rights of others. Before adopting a new trademark, entrepreneurs should conduct a thorough search to ensure that the mark is not already in use by another business. They should also monitor their trademark for unauthorized use and take action against infringers.

Another challenge is protecting trademarks in the international marketplace. Trademark protection varies from country to country, and entrepreneurs doing business internationally must understand the legal requirements in each jurisdiction.

Trademark law is a critical area of law for entrepreneurs, as it protects their valuable marks and gives them a competitive advantage in the marketplace. By understanding the basics of trademark law and working with legal professionals, entrepreneurs can ensure that their marks are protected and avoid legal disputes related to infringement.

2.4 Licensing and Contract Considerations

Licensing and contract considerations are an important aspect of intellectual property law for entrepreneurs. Entrepreneurs often need to license their intellectual property to others or enter into contracts that involve the use of intellectual property, and it's essential to ensure that the terms of these agreements protect their interests.

Licensing is the process of granting permission to use intellectual property, such as patents, trademarks, or copyrights, in exchange for compensation. Licensing agreements typically specify the rights and limitations of the licensee, as well as the compensation structure and any conditions or restrictions on the use of the intellectual property. Licensing agreements can be complex and may require legal assistance to ensure that they are properly drafted and enforceable.

Contract considerations also come into play when dealing with intellectual property. For example, an entrepreneur may enter into a contract with a vendor or supplier that involves the use of intellectual property, such as software or a trademarked name. These contracts should include provisions that protect the entrepreneur's rights to the intellectual property, such as confidentiality provisions, indemnification clauses, and limitations on the use of the intellectual property.

Another important consideration is ownership of intellectual property created by employees or contractors. In general, an entrepreneur or business is considered the owner of intellectual property created by employees in the scope of their employment. However, the rules regarding ownership can be complex, and entrepreneurs should have policies and agreements in place to clarify ownership and ensure that their interests are protected.

Licensing and contract considerations are critical aspects of intellectual property law for entrepreneurs. By understanding the legal requirements and working with legal professionals to ensure that their agreements are properly drafted and enforceable, entrepreneurs can protect their valuable intellectual property and avoid legal disputes related to licensing and contracts.

Chapter 3: Employment Law

Chapter 3 focuses on employment law, which is a complex area of law that governs the relationship between employers and employees. For entrepreneurs, employment law is a critical consideration, as it affects hiring practices, employee relations, and compliance with various legal requirements.

Employment law covers a wide range of issues, including discrimination, harassment, wages and hours, leave policies, benefits, and termination of employment. Entrepreneurs must be aware of their obligations under federal, state, and local employment laws and ensure that their employment policies and practices comply with these laws.

Entrepreneurs must also consider the impact of employment law on their business operations and culture. Effective management of employees requires a solid understanding of employment law, as well as a commitment to creating a positive and inclusive workplace culture that supports employee satisfaction and productivity.

We will explore the key legal considerations related to employment law, including the legal requirements for hiring and firing employees, the importance of effective employee management and communication, and the legal requirements related to employee compensation and benefits. We will also explore the importance of maintaining compliance with employment laws and regulations and the potential consequences of noncompliance.

Understanding employment law is essential for entrepreneurs to create a successful and compliant business that attracts and retains talented employees. By mastering the legal requirements and best practices related to employment law, entrepreneurs can build a positive workplace culture that supports their business goals and enhances their reputation in the marketplace.

3.1 Understanding Employment Law

Employment law is a complex and ever-changing area of law that governs the relationship between employers and employees. As an entrepreneur, it's essential to have a solid understanding of employment law and the legal requirements that apply to your business.

One of the key aspects of employment law is understanding the legal requirements for hiring and firing employees. This includes compliance with anti-discrimination laws, such as Title VII of the Civil Rights Act, the Americans with Disabilities Act (ADA), and the Age Discrimination in Employment Act (ADEA). These laws prohibit discrimination in hiring and firing decisions based on protected characteristics such as race, color, national origin, sex, religion, disability, and age.

Entrepreneurs must also be aware of the legal requirements related to employee classification, including the distinction between employees and independent contractors. Misclassifying employees as independent contractors can lead to significant legal and financial consequences, including liability for unpaid taxes and benefits.

Effective employee management and communication are also important aspects of employment law. This includes creating and enforcing policies related to workplace conduct, harassment and discrimination prevention, and employee leave and accommodation requests. Entrepreneurs should also ensure that their employees are trained on these policies and understand their rights and responsibilities in the workplace.

Finally, entrepreneurs must be aware of the legal requirements related to employee compensation and benefits, including minimum wage and overtime laws, employee benefits, and compliance with the Fair Labor Standards Act (FLSA). Failure to comply with these requirements can lead to legal disputes and financial penalties.

Understanding employment law is essential for entrepreneurs to create a successful and compliant business. By mastering the legal requirements and best practices related to employment law, entrepreneurs can create a positive workplace culture that supports their business goals and enhances their reputation in the marketplace.

3.2 Hiring Employees: The Hiring Process

Hiring employees is a critical step for entrepreneurs who are looking to grow their business. However, the hiring process can also be fraught with legal risks and compliance considerations.

To minimize legal risks and ensure compliance with applicable employment laws, entrepreneurs should follow a structured and consistent hiring process. This process should begin with a clear job description that outlines the essential functions of the position, the qualifications and experience required, and any other relevant factors, such as physical or environmental requirements.

The next step is to create a recruitment plan that identifies the sources of potential candidates, such as online job boards, social media, employee referrals, or recruiting firms. It's important to ensure that the recruitment plan does not discriminate against any protected categories of employees, such as race, gender, age, religion, or disability.

Once a pool of candidates has been identified, entrepreneurs should conduct interviews that are structured and consistent, asking the same set of questions to each candidate. It's important to avoid asking questions that may be perceived as discriminatory or that violate privacy laws, such as questions about an applicant's age, marital status, or medical history.

After the interviews have been completed, entrepreneurs should conduct background checks and reference checks to verify the candidate's employment history, education, and other relevant information. It's important to obtain written consent from the candidate before conducting any background or credit checks, and to comply with applicable laws related to criminal history and credit checks.

Entrepreneurs should make a job offer to the selected candidate, including a written offer letter that outlines the terms of the employment, such as compensation, benefits, and other relevant terms. It's important to ensure that the job offer does not violate any applicable employment laws, such as minimum wage or overtime laws, or discrimination laws.

The hiring process is a critical step for entrepreneurs who are looking to grow their business. By following a structured and consistent process and ensuring compliance with applicable employment laws, entrepreneurs can attract and hire top talent while minimizing legal risks and ensuring a positive workplace culture.

3.3 Employee Benefits and Compensation

Employee benefits and compensation are important considerations for entrepreneurs who are looking to attract and retain top talent. There are a variety of employee benefits and compensation options available, and entrepreneurs should consider their budget, business needs, and legal requirements when designing their benefits and compensation packages. One of the most important aspects of employee compensation is ensuring compliance with applicable minimum wage and overtime laws. Entrepreneurs should ensure that all employees are paid at least the minimum wage required by law and that eligible employees are paid overtime for any hours worked beyond 40 hours per week. Failure to comply with minimum wage and overtime laws can result in legal liability and reputational harm for the business.

In addition to minimum wage and overtime laws, entrepreneurs should also consider other forms of employee compensation, such as bonuses, commissions, and profit-sharing plans. These forms of compensation can be used to incentivize and reward employees for achieving specific performance goals or contributing to the overall success of the business.

Employee benefits are another important consideration for entrepreneurs. Common employee benefits include health insurance, retirement plans, and paid time off. Entrepreneurs should consider the needs and preferences of their workforce when designing their employee benefits packages, as well as any legal requirements related to employee benefits.

For example, the Affordable Care Act (ACA) requires certain employers to offer health insurance to their employees or face penalties. Similarly, the

Family and Medical Leave Act (FMLA) requires certain employers to offer unpaid leave to eligible employees for certain medical and family-related reasons.

Employee benefits and compensation are important considerations for entrepreneurs who are looking to attract and retain top talent. By ensuring compliance with applicable laws and designing packages that meet the needs and preferences of their workforce, entrepreneurs can build a positive workplace culture and achieve long-term business success.

3.4 Employee Termination

Employee termination is a difficult and sensitive issue for entrepreneurs, but it is an important part of managing a workforce. There are a variety of reasons why an entrepreneur may need to terminate an employee, including poor performance, violation of company policies, or budget cuts.

Regardless of the reason for termination, entrepreneurs should follow best practices to ensure that the process is fair, legal, and respectful of the employee. This includes giving the employee clear and specific reasons for their termination and providing them with an opportunity to improve their performance or address any concerns before termination.

In addition to providing clear reasons for termination, entrepreneurs should also ensure that they are in compliance with all applicable laws and regulations. For example, the Worker Adjustment and Retraining Notification (WARN) Act requires certain employers to provide advance notice of mass layoffs or plant closings.

Another important consideration for entrepreneurs is the documentation of the termination process. Entrepreneurs should keep detailed records of any disciplinary actions, performance evaluations, or other factors that contributed to the termination decision. This documentation can help protect the business from legal liability in the event of a wrongful termination lawsuit.

Entrepreneurs should be prepared to handle the emotional and practical aspects of employee termination. This includes ensuring that the terminated employee has access to any necessary resources, such as counseling services or assistance with finding a new job.

Employee termination is a difficult but necessary part of managing a workforce. By following best practices and ensuring compliance with applicable laws and regulations, entrepreneurs can minimize legal risk and maintain a positive workplace culture.

Chapter 4: Tax Law

As an entrepreneur, understanding tax law is essential for running a successful business. Tax obligations can have a significant impact on a company's bottom line, and failure to comply with tax laws can result in serious consequences, such as penalties, fines, or even legal action.

Chapter 4 will provide an overview of tax law, including the different types of taxes that entrepreneurs may be required to pay, such as income tax, payroll tax, and sales tax. It will also cover important considerations related to tax compliance, including record-keeping, filing deadlines, and tax deductions.

Entrepreneurs will also learn about common tax issues that they may face, such as how to classify employees vs. independent contractors, the tax implications of owning and selling property, and how to navigate tax audits.

By understanding tax law and complying with tax obligations, entrepreneurs can minimize their tax liability, maintain compliance with applicable laws and regulations, and ensure the financial health of their business.

4.1 Understanding Tax Law

Tax law is a complex and constantly evolving area of law that governs the taxation of individuals and businesses. As an entrepreneur, it's important to have a basic understanding of tax law in order to comply with tax obligations and minimize your tax liability.

One of the key concepts to understand in tax law is the difference between tax planning and tax evasion. Tax planning involves taking advantage of legal tax deductions and credits in order to reduce your tax liability. Tax evasion, on the other hand, involves intentionally failing to report income or taking illegal actions to avoid paying taxes.

It's important to note that tax planning is legal and encouraged, while tax evasion is illegal and can result in serious consequences, including fines, penalties, and even criminal charges.

Another important aspect of tax law for entrepreneurs is understanding the different types of taxes that may apply to their business. Some common types of taxes include income tax, payroll tax, sales tax, and property tax.

Income tax is a tax on the income earned by an individual or business, while payroll tax is a tax on the wages and salaries paid to employees. Sales tax is a tax on the sale of goods and services, and property tax is a tax on the value of real property, such as land and buildings.

Entrepreneurs should also be aware of the various tax credits and deductions that may be available to them. For example, businesses may be eligible for deductions for expenses such as employee wages, rent, and office supplies. There are also tax credits available for certain activities, such as research and development.

Understanding tax law is essential for entrepreneurs who want to run a successful and compliant business. By staying informed and working with a tax professional when necessary, entrepreneurs can navigate the complexities of tax law and minimize their tax liability.

4.2 Tax Planning and Strategies for Entrepreneurs

Tax planning is an important part of running a successful business, and there are many strategies that entrepreneurs can use to minimize their tax liability. By understanding the tax code and working with a tax professional, entrepreneurs can identify opportunities for tax savings and take advantage of them.

One common tax planning strategy for entrepreneurs is to take advantage of deductions and credits. This might involve deducting expenses such as office rent, equipment purchases, and employee wages. There are also tax credits available for certain activities, such as research and development.

Another strategy is to consider the structure of your business. Different types of businesses are taxed differently, and choosing the right structure can help you reduce your tax liability. For example, forming a limited liability company (LLC) or an S corporation can provide tax benefits, as these structures are taxed differently from sole proprietorships and partnerships.

Entrepreneurs should also be aware of the tax implications of their business activities. For example, selling a business or property can have significant tax consequences. By understanding the tax implications of these activities, entrepreneurs can make informed decisions that minimize their tax liability.

In addition to these strategies, it's important for entrepreneurs to stay informed about changes to the tax code. Tax laws and regulations are constantly evolving, and staying up-to-date on these changes can help entrepreneurs stay compliant and take advantage of new opportunities for tax savings.

Tax planning is an important part of running a successful business. By working with a tax professional and taking advantage of tax planning strategies, entrepreneurs can minimize their tax liability and ensure the financial health of their business.

4.3 Tax Compliance

As an entrepreneur, it's important to be in compliance with tax laws and regulations. Failure to comply with tax laws can result in penalties, fines, and other legal consequences, which can be damaging to your business's reputation and financial health. Here are some key considerations for tax compliance:

Know your tax obligations:

Knowing your tax obligations is a critical aspect of tax compliance. As an entrepreneur, you are responsible for paying taxes on your business income, which includes both federal and state taxes. Here are some key considerations for understanding your tax obligations:

Federal taxes:

If you are operating a business in the United States, you are required to pay federal taxes on your business income. The type of federal tax you pay depends on the legal structure of your business. For example, if you operate a sole proprietorship, you are required to pay self-employment tax on your business income. If you operate a corporation, you are required to pay corporate income tax on your business income. It's important to understand the type of federal tax you are required to pay and to ensure that you are paying it on time.

State taxes:

In addition to federal taxes, you may also be required to pay state taxes on your business income. The type of state tax you pay depends on the state in which your business is located. For example, if you operate a business in California, you are required to pay state income tax on your business income. It's important to understand the type of state tax you are required to pay and to ensure that you are paying it on time.

Sales tax:

If you sell goods or services, you may also be required to collect and remit sales tax to the appropriate state or local tax authority. The rules for collecting and remitting sales tax vary by state, so it's important to understand the rules in your state and to ensure that you are in compliance with them.

Employment taxes:

If you have employees, you are also responsible for paying employment taxes, which include Social Security and Medicare taxes, federal unemployment taxes, and state unemployment taxes. It's important to understand your obligations for paying these taxes and to ensure that you are paying them on time.

By understanding your tax obligations, you can ensure that you are in compliance with tax laws and regulations and avoid penalties and fines. It's important to stay up to date on changes to tax laws and regulations and to work with a tax professional to ensure that you are in compliance with all of your tax obligations.

Keep accurate records:

Keeping accurate records is an essential part of tax compliance and overall business management.

Here are some key considerations for keeping accurate records:

Business income and expenses:

You should keep track of all income and expenses related to your business, including sales, receipts, invoices, and bills. This information will be used to calculate your business income and expenses for tax purposes.

Business assets:

You should also keep track of any assets that you acquire for your business, such as equipment, inventory, or property. This information will be used to calculate depreciation and other tax deductions related to your business assets.

Employee records:

If you have employees, you should keep accurate records of their wages, hours worked, and any benefits or compensation provided. This information will be used to calculate employment taxes and to comply with various employment laws and regulations.

Tax documents:

You should keep copies of all tax-related documents, including tax returns, tax payments, and any correspondence with tax authorities. This information will be used to support your tax filings and to respond to any questions or inquiries from tax authorities.

By keeping accurate records, you can ensure that you are in compliance with tax laws and regulations and that you have the information you need to make informed business decisions. It's important to establish a record-keeping system that works for your business and to update it regularly. You may also want to work with a bookkeeper or accountant to ensure that your records are accurate and up to date.

File your tax returns on time:

Filing your tax returns on time is an important aspect of tax compliance.

Here are some key things to keep in mind:

Due dates:

It's important to know the due dates for your tax returns and to make sure that you file them on time. For example, for federal income tax returns, the due date is generally April 15th of each year. However, due to various circumstances, the due date may be extended, so it's important to stay up-to-date on any changes.

Extensions:

If you are unable to file your tax return by the due date, you may be able to request an extension. This will give you additional time to file your return, but it doesn't give you extra time to pay any taxes owed. You'll still need to estimate and pay any taxes owed by the original due date to avoid penalties and interest.

Penalties and interest:

If you fail to file your tax return on time, you may be subject to penalties and interest. The penalty for late filing is typically 5% of the unpaid tax for each month or part of a month that the return is late, up to a maximum of 25%. Interest is also charged on any unpaid tax from the due date of the return until it is paid in full.

Tax refunds:

If you are due a tax refund, it's in your best interest to file your tax return as soon as possible. The sooner you file, the sooner you'll receive your refund. In addition, if you don't file your return within three years of the due date, you may forfeit your right to a refund.

By filing your tax returns on time, you can avoid penalties and interest, ensure that you receive any tax refunds you're owed, and maintain good standing with tax authorities. If you're unsure about when your tax returns are due or have questions about filing requirements, it's a good idea to consult with a tax professional.

Work with a tax professional:

Working with a tax professional is an important part of managing your tax obligations as an entrepreneur.

Here are some reasons why it's a good idea to consider hiring a tax professional:

Expertise:

Tax professionals are trained and experienced in tax law and regulations, so they can help you navigate complex tax issues and make sure you are complying with all relevant requirements. They can also help you take advantage of tax benefits and deductions that you may not be aware of.

Time-saving:

Managing your taxes can be time-consuming, especially if you're not familiar with tax laws and regulations. By working with a tax professional, you can save time and focus on running your business while they handle your tax obligations.

Reduce errors:

Filing taxes can be complicated, and making mistakes can lead to penalties and interest. Tax professionals are trained to be meticulous and ensure that your tax returns are accurate and complete.

Audit assistance:

In the event of an audit, a tax professional can help you navigate the process and provide guidance on what documentation you need to provide. They can also represent you before the tax authorities and help you resolve any issues that arise.

When looking for a tax professional, it's important to do your research and find someone who is knowledgeable and experienced in your specific industry or business. You may also want to consider their fees and the level of service they offer. By working with a tax professional, you can ensure that you are managing your tax obligations effectively and reducing the risk of costly mistakes

---

Stay informed:

Staying informed about changes in tax laws and regulations is crucial for entrepreneurs, as it can impact their tax obligations and the bottom line of their business. Here are some ways to stay informed about tax-related updates:

Consult with a tax professional:

A tax professional can keep you up-to-date with changes in tax laws and regulations that may affect your business. They can also provide advice on how to comply with new tax requirements and take advantage of tax breaks.

Attend seminars and conferences:

Attending tax seminars and conferences is an excellent way to stay informed about new tax developments. These events often feature presentations from experts in the field and provide opportunities to ask questions and network with other business owners.

Subscribe to tax-related publications:

There are many publications, such as tax newsletters and journals, that provide regular updates on tax laws and regulations. Subscribing to these publications can help you stay current on changes in tax law and provide insights into how these changes may affect your business.

Use online resources:

The internet is a valuable resource for staying informed about tax-related updates. The IRS website, for example, provides information on tax law changes, forms and instructions, and other helpful resources. There are also online tax communities and forums where business owners can share information and ask questions.

By staying informed about changes in tax laws and regulations, entrepreneurs can ensure that they are complying with tax requirements and taking advantage of tax benefits. It can also help them avoid penalties and interest and ultimately, save money for their business.

Tax compliance is essential for the success of your business. By understanding your tax obligations, keeping accurate records, filing your tax returns on time, working with a tax professional, and staying informed about changes to tax laws and regulations, you can ensure compliance and avoid penalties and fines.

4.4 Tax Audits and Appeals

Tax audits and appeals are a part of the tax compliance process, and it's important for entrepreneurs to understand how to handle them. Here are some things to keep in mind:

Be prepared:

Being prepared is key to effectively navigating a tax audit or appeal. Before the audit or appeal, review your tax returns and supporting documents to ensure that they are accurate and complete. This includes double-checking calculations, ensuring that all income and deductions are properly reported, and verifying that you have all necessary supporting documentation.

It is also important to be prepared to answer questions from the auditor or appeal officer. Make sure you understand the basis of any adjustments being proposed and have a clear explanation for any discrepancies. Keep in mind that being cooperative and transparent can often help resolve issues more quickly and with less hassle.

Consider seeking the advice of a tax professional or attorney who has experience in tax audits and appeals. They can help you prepare for the process, provide guidance on how to address any issues that arise, and represent you during the audit or appeal.

Cooperate with the auditor:

When you are being audited, it is important to cooperate with the auditor to the best of your ability. This means providing the auditor with any requested documents and information in a timely manner, and being responsive to their questions.

By cooperating with the auditor, you can demonstrate that you are taking the audit seriously and that you are committed to resolving any issues that may arise. In addition, being cooperative can often help to establish a positive working relationship with the auditor, which can be beneficial if any disputes arise during the audit.

It is also important to remember that you have certain rights as a taxpayer during an audit. For example, you have the right to be represented by a tax professional or attorney, and you have the right to appeal any proposed adjustments.

If you have concerns about the conduct of the auditor or feel that your rights are being violated, it is important to speak up and raise these issues with the auditor or their supervisor. By working together and maintaining open lines of communication, you may be able to resolve any issues more quickly and with less stress.

Consider hiring a tax professional:

When it comes to navigating the complex landscape of tax law, many entrepreneurs find it helpful to work with a tax professional. A tax professional can help you understand your tax obligations, identify tax planning opportunities, and ensure that you are in compliance with all relevant tax laws and regulations.

There are several different types of tax professionals that you can work with, including certified public accountants (CPAs), tax attorneys, and enrolled agents. Each of these professionals has a unique set of skills and qualifications, and the type of professional that you choose may depend on your specific needs and circumstances.

For example, if you have a particularly complex tax situation or are facing an audit or other tax dispute, you may want to consider working with a tax attorney. On the other hand, if you are primarily concerned with tax planning and compliance, a CPA or enrolled agent may be a better fit.

When hiring a tax professional, it is important to do your research and choose someone who is experienced, knowledgeable, and trustworthy. You may want to ask for referrals from other entrepreneurs or business owners, and you should always check the credentials and references of any potential candidates.

Working with a tax professional can be an investment, but it can also provide valuable peace of mind and help you avoid costly mistakes or penalties down the line.

Understand your appeal rights:

If you are audited by the IRS or another tax authority and disagree with the findings, you may have the right to appeal the decision. Understanding your appeal rights can be an important part of navigating the tax audit process and ensuring that you are treated fairly.

The specific appeal rights that you have will depend on the type of audit and the tax authority involved. In general, however, you may have the right to request a conference with an appeals officer, submit additional documentation or evidence, and challenge any penalties or fees that have been assessed.

To exercise your appeal rights, you will typically need to follow a specific process and meet certain deadlines. It is important to carefully review any audit findings or notices that you receive and to consult with a tax professional if you are unsure of how to proceed.

In some cases, it may be possible to resolve a tax dispute through mediation or other alternative dispute resolution methods. These approaches can be less formal and costly than traditional appeals processes, and may be a good option if you are looking to resolve the issue quickly and efficiently.

Regardless of the specific approach that you take, it is important to understand your appeal rights and to work with a tax professional who can help you navigate the process effectively. By doing so, you can increase your chances of a successful outcome and minimize the impact of a tax audit on your business.

Be aware of potential penalties:

When dealing with tax audits and appeals, it is important to be aware of the potential penalties that may be imposed by tax authorities. These penalties can include interest charges, fines, and even criminal charges in some cases.

To avoid potential penalties, it is important to be proactive in your tax compliance efforts. This means keeping accurate records, filing your tax returns on time, and working with a tax professional to ensure that you are meeting all of your tax obligations.

If you are facing a tax audit or appeal, it is important to understand your rights and options. This may include the option to appeal the audit decision, or to negotiate a settlement with the tax authorities.

In any case, it is important to take the matter seriously and to cooperate with the tax authorities as much as possible. This can help to mitigate potential penalties and to resolve the issue as quickly and effectively as possible.

By understanding how to handle tax audits and appeals, entrepreneurs can better protect their businesses from potential tax liabilities and penalties. By keeping accurate records, cooperating with auditors, and seeking professional advice when necessary, they can ensure that they are complying with tax laws and regulations and avoiding unnecessary risks.

Chapter 5: Contract Law

Chapter 5: Contract Law will focus on the legal principles and considerations surrounding contracts for entrepreneurs. Contracts are an essential aspect of any business operation, and understanding the legal framework behind them is crucial for success.

In this chapter, we will explore the key concepts of contract law, including the different types of contracts, the elements of a valid contract, and the legal implications of breaches of contract. We will also delve into important considerations when drafting and negotiating contracts, including the use of standard contract clauses, the importance of clear and unambiguous language, and the role of attorneys in the contract process.

By the end of this chapter, readers will have a solid understanding of the legal principles that govern contracts, and will be better equipped to navigate the contract process in their own business operations.

5.1 Basics of Contract Law

Contracts are a fundamental aspect of business transactions, and understanding the basic principles of contract law is essential for entrepreneurs. In this section, we will cover the foundational principles of contract law, including the different types of contracts, the elements of a valid contract, and the consequences of a breach of contract.

One of the key aspects of contract law is the distinction between express and implied contracts. An express contract is one where the terms of the agreement are explicitly stated, either in writing or orally. An implied contract, on the other hand, is one where the terms of the agreement are inferred from the conduct of the parties involved.

To be legally binding, a contract must contain certain elements. These include an offer, acceptance, consideration, and mutual assent. An offer is a proposal by one party to enter into a contract with another party. Acceptance is the agreement by the other party to the terms of the offer. Consideration is something of value that is exchanged by the parties, such as money or services. Finally, mutual assent refers to the agreement of both parties to enter into the contract voluntarily and with full understanding of the terms.

If one party breaches a contract, there are a variety of legal remedies available to the other party. These may include specific performance (i.e., requiring the breaching party to fulfill their contractual obligations), monetary damages, or rescission (i.e., termination) of the contract.

Having a solid understanding of the basics of contract law is essential for entrepreneurs who want to ensure that their business transactions are legally binding and enforceable.

5.2 Types of Contracts

There are several types of contracts that entrepreneurs should be aware of when conducting business. These include:

Express Contracts:

These are contracts that are explicitly stated, either in writing or orally. Both parties agree to the terms of the contract and sign a document that outlines these terms.

Implied Contracts:

These contracts are not explicitly stated, but are implied by the actions of both parties. For example, if a customer enters a restaurant and orders food, an implied contract is formed between the customer and the restaurant that the customer will pay for the food they ordered.

Unilateral Contracts:

These are contracts where one party makes a promise in exchange for an action from the other party. For example, if an entrepreneur offers a reward for anyone who finds their lost dog, this is a unilateral contract.

Bilateral Contracts:

These are contracts where both parties make promises to each other. For example, if an entrepreneur hires an employee, the entrepreneur promises to pay the employee a salary in exchange for the employee's work.

Executed Contracts:

These are contracts that have been fully performed by both parties.

Executory Contracts:

These are contracts where one or both parties have not yet fully performed their obligations.

Understanding the different types of contracts can help entrepreneurs draft contracts that accurately reflect their agreements and avoid disputes.

5.3 Key Contract Terms and Conditions

These terms are critical to ensuring that all parties are on the same page and that the contract is legally enforceable.

Some of the key terms and conditions that should be included in a contract are:

Parties Involved:

Parties involved is a crucial aspect of any contract, as it defines the individuals or entities who are entering into the agreement. It is essential to identify and clearly state the parties involved to avoid confusion or ambiguity in the future.

In a contract, parties can be individuals, corporations, partnerships, or other legal entities. It is important to clearly identify the parties involved by their legal names, addresses, and contact information. This information should be accurate and up to date.

It is also essential to define the roles and responsibilities of each party in the contract. This includes outlining the obligations, rights, and duties of each party, as well as any limitations or restrictions. The terms of the contract should be clear and concise, to avoid any misunderstandings or disputes later on.

It is advisable to seek legal advice when drafting or negotiating contracts, especially when dealing with complex arrangements. An attorney can help ensure that the parties involved are accurately identified and that the terms and conditions of the contract are legally binding and enforceable.

Scope of Work:

In the context of a contract, the scope of work refers to the specific tasks, deliverables, and services that the parties have agreed upon. It outlines what each party is responsible for and what they will deliver or receive.

The scope of work should be clearly defined in the contract to avoid misunderstandings and disagreements later on. It should be detailed enough to ensure that both parties have a clear understanding of the work to be performed and the expected outcomes.

When defining the scope of work, it is important to consider the following:

- The purpose of the contract: The scope of work should align with the overall purpose of the contract and clearly state the desired outcome.

- Deliverables: The scope of work should specify the exact deliverables that are expected from each party. This includes any reports, products, or services that are to be provided.

- Timeline: The scope of work should outline the expected timeline for the completion of each deliverable and the project as a whole.

- Budget: The scope of work should specify the budget and payment terms for the project.

- Changes to scope: The scope of work should include provisions for making changes to the scope of work, including how changes will be requested, evaluated, and approved.

Defining the scope of work is an essential part of creating a contract that clearly outlines the expectations and responsibilities of each party. It ensures that everyone is on the same page and helps to minimize the risk of disputes or misunderstandings.

Payment Terms:

payment terms are an important aspect of any contract. They outline the amount of money to be paid, when it is due, and any conditions that must be met before payment can be made. Payment terms can vary depending on the type of contract and the nature of the work being performed. For example, in a construction contract, payment may be tied to the completion of certain milestones, while in a service contract, payment may be made upon completion of the work.

It is important to clearly define payment terms in a contract to avoid misunderstandings or disputes. This includes outlining the amount of the payment, the due date, and any late payment fees or interest charges. In addition, the contract should specify the method of payment, such as cash, check, wire transfer, or credit card.

It is also important to consider any potential issues that may arise with payment, such as disputes over the quality of work performed or disagreements over additional charges. Including a dispute resolution clause in the contract can help to address these issues and provide a clear process for resolving any disputes that may arise.

Term and Termination:

In a contract, it is important to define the term, or duration, of the agreement. This specifies the period of time during which the parties are obligated to fulfill their obligations under the contract. The termination provisions of the contract describe the circumstances under which the agreement can be ended before the end of the term. These provisions can include events such as breach of contract, bankruptcy, or mutual agreement between the parties.

For example, a contract between a landlord and a tenant may have a term of one year, with the option to renew for additional one-year terms. The termination provision may state that the landlord has the right to terminate the agreement if the tenant fails to pay rent for a certain period of time, or if the tenant violates certain terms of the lease.

It is important to carefully consider the term and termination provisions of a contract to ensure that they align with the goals and expectations of the parties involved.

Confidentiality and Non-Disclosure:

Confidentiality and non-disclosure clauses are often included in contracts to protect the sensitive information shared between the parties. These clauses set out the terms and conditions for how confidential information will be treated and what steps must be taken to protect it from unauthorized disclosure or use.

The confidentiality clause generally defines what information is considered confidential and how it can be used. It may require the recipient to keep the information secret and to not use it for any other purpose than the purpose specified in the contract. The clause may also set out the circumstances under which the confidentiality obligations will no longer apply, such as if the information becomes public knowledge through no fault of the recipient.

A non-disclosure clause is often included in employment contracts to prohibit employees from disclosing confidential information about the company or its clients. This clause may also apply to third-party contractors who work with the company. Non-disclosure clauses may also include provisions that require the return or destruction of confidential information upon termination of the contract or employment.

It is important to carefully consider the scope of these clauses and ensure that they are tailored to the specific needs of the parties and the nature of the information being shared. In some cases, it may also be appropriate to include provisions for remedies or damages in the event of a breach of confidentiality or non-disclosure.

Warranties and Representations:

In a contract, warranties and representations refer to the promises made by one party to the other about the quality, performance, or characteristics of a product or service.

Warranties are guarantees that the product or service will meet certain standards or will perform in a particular way. For example, a software company might warrant that their product is free of bugs and will operate correctly under normal conditions. If the product does not meet the stated warranty, the company may be required to provide a remedy, such as repairing or replacing the product.

Representations, on the other hand, are statements made by one party to the other about a particular aspect of the transaction or relationship. For example, in a business sale agreement, the seller may represent that all financial statements provided to the buyer are accurate and complete. If the representation is later found to be untrue, the buyer may have a claim for damages.

Warranties and representations are important terms in a contract because they help to define the expectations of the parties and provide a means for resolving disputes if those expectations are not met. It is important to carefully consider the language used to describe warranties and representations in a contract to ensure that they are clear, specific, and enforceable.

Dispute Resolution:

Dispute resolution is a crucial aspect of any contract, as it outlines how the parties will handle any disagreements that may arise during the performance of the contract. There are several different methods of dispute resolution that may be included in a contract, including mediation, arbitration, and litigation.

Mediation involves a neutral third party, the mediator, who helps the parties to negotiate and reach a mutually acceptable resolution. Mediation is often less formal and less costly than other forms of dispute resolution. Arbitration is a more formal process where a neutral third party, the arbitrator, hears evidence and makes a binding decision. Arbitration is often quicker and less expensive than litigation but may not provide the same level of due process.

Litigation is the most formal and expensive method of dispute resolution, involving a court proceeding where a judge or jury decides the outcome. Litigation can be time-consuming and costly, but may provide a more robust legal process and more formal resolution than other methods.

When drafting a contract, it is essential to carefully consider the best method of dispute resolution for the specific situation and to clearly outline the process in the contract. Additionally, it is essential to consider any applicable laws and regulations regarding dispute resolution, such as mandatory arbitration clauses in certain industries or jurisdictions.

Including these key terms and conditions in a contract can help to ensure that all parties are on the same page and that the contract is legally enforceable.

5.4 Contract Disputes and Resolution

Contract disputes can arise when one party fails to meet their obligations under the contract, or when there is a disagreement about the interpretation of certain terms or conditions. When a contract dispute occurs, it is important to try to resolve the issue as quickly and efficiently as possible, in order to minimize any potential damage to the business relationship.

There are several methods for resolving contract disputes, including:

- Negotiation: This involves direct communication between the parties in order to try to reach a mutually acceptable resolution.

- Mediation: A neutral third party is brought in to help facilitate negotiations between the parties and reach a settlement.

- Arbitration: This involves a neutral third party who listens to both sides and makes a binding decision.

- Litigation: This is the process of resolving disputes through the court system.

The best method for resolving a contract dispute will depend on the specific circumstances of the situation. It is important to carefully consider the potential costs and benefits of each approach, as well as the likelihood of success.

In any contract dispute, it is important to have a clear understanding of the terms of the contract and to document all communication related to the dispute. It may also be helpful to consult with a legal professional who specializes in contract law to help navigate the dispute resolution process.

Chapter 6: Business Formation and Governance

Chapter 6 of this guide is focused on the topic of Business Formation and Governance. This chapter explores the different types of business entities that entrepreneurs can choose from when starting a business, as well as the various legal and regulatory requirements that must be met to establish and maintain a business. Additionally, this chapter covers important considerations related to the governance of a business, including the role of directors and officers, shareholder agreements, and corporate compliance. By understanding the fundamentals of business formation and governance, entrepreneurs can make informed decisions and take the necessary steps to establish and maintain a successful business.

6.1 Choosing a Business Entity

When starting a business, one of the most important decisions you will make is choosing the type of legal entity your business will operate as. There are several types of entities to choose from, including sole proprietorship, partnership, limited liability company (LLC), corporation, and cooperative. Each type of entity has its own advantages and disadvantages in terms of liability protection, tax implications, management structure, and ease of formation. It's important to choose the entity that best fits your specific business needs and goals.

Sole proprietorships and partnerships are the simplest and least expensive types of entities to form, but they offer no protection for personal assets and can expose owners to unlimited liability for business debts and legal claims. LLCs and corporations offer limited liability protection, which can shield personal assets from business debts and legal claims, but they are more complex and expensive to form and operate. Co-operatives are typically used for businesses that are owned and operated by their members, such as agricultural co-ops or credit unions.

Choosing the right entity for your business requires careful consideration of a variety of factors, such as the size and nature of your business, the number of owners, and your tax and liability concerns. It's important to consult with an attorney and accountant when making this decision to ensure that you fully understand the legal and financial implications of each option.

6.2 Formation and Registration

Once you have decided on the type of business entity you want to form, the next step is to actually form and register your business. This involves filing the appropriate paperwork with the state government, obtaining any necessary licenses and permits, and complying with any other legal requirements.

The specific steps involved in forming and registering a business will depend on the type of entity you have chosen and the state in which you are doing business. For example, if you are forming a corporation, you will typically need to file articles of incorporation with the state and obtain a corporate charter. If you are forming an LLC, you will need to file articles of organization and an operating agreement.

It is important to ensure that you complete all necessary paperwork and comply with all legal requirements when forming and registering your business. Failure to do so can result in legal and financial consequences, including fines, penalties, and even the dissolution of your business.

6.3 Corporate Governance

Corporate governance refers to the system of rules, practices, and processes by which a company is directed and controlled. It includes the mechanisms and relationships used by a company to manage and direct its business affairs, and is essential to ensuring that the company is run in a fair, transparent, and accountable manner.

Some key aspects of corporate governance include the composition and role of the board of directors, the responsibilities of executive management, and the various committees and policies that guide decision-making and oversight within the company. Good corporate governance practices help to minimize the risk of corporate misconduct, fraud, and other abuses, and can also enhance a company's reputation and performance.

In addition to legal and regulatory requirements, companies may also be subject to various codes of conduct, industry standards, and best practices that govern their governance practices. It is important for businesses to establish and maintain effective corporate governance systems that align with their values and goals, and to regularly review and update these systems as needed to ensure their ongoing effectiveness.

6.4 Shareholders' Agreements and Other Corporate Documents

In Chapter 6, we also explore the importance of shareholders' agreements and other corporate documents in corporate governance. A shareholders' agreement is a contract between the shareholders of a corporation that outlines their rights and responsibilities in relation to the corporation. It can cover a range of issues, including the management and direction of the corporation, the issuance and transfer of shares, and the rights of minority shareholders.

Other important corporate documents include bylaws, which set out the rules and procedures for running the corporation, and articles of incorporation or articles of organization, which are the documents filed with the state to create the corporation or LLC.

These documents are essential for clarifying the relationships and responsibilities between shareholders and management, and for ensuring that the corporation operates effectively and in compliance with applicable laws and regulations. It is important to have these documents drafted and reviewed by a qualified attorney to ensure that they meet the specific needs and objectives of the corporation and its shareholders.

Chapter 7: Compliance and Risk Management

Chapter 7 of the business law guide focuses on compliance and risk management. Compliance refers to the adherence to laws, regulations, and ethical practices that govern business operations. Risk management refers to the identification, assessment, and mitigation of potential risks that a business may face.

In this chapter, we will cover the importance of compliance and risk management for businesses, as well as strategies for developing and implementing effective compliance and risk management programs. We will also discuss key legal and regulatory requirements that businesses must comply with, such as data privacy laws and anti-discrimination laws, and explore ways to minimize and mitigate risks related to areas such as contracts, intellectual property, and employment.

7.1 Regulatory Compliance Overview

Regulatory compliance refers to the process of ensuring that a business is operating in accordance with the laws, rules, and regulations set forth by the relevant regulatory agencies. This can include compliance with environmental regulations, workplace safety regulations, data privacy regulations, financial regulations, and more, depending on the nature of the business.

Compliance is important for several reasons. Firstly, failure to comply with regulations can result in significant legal and financial penalties, as well as damage to a company's reputation. Additionally, compliance can help to improve operational efficiency and reduce the risk of accidents or other incidents that could harm employees or the public.

To ensure compliance, businesses should establish clear policies and procedures, conduct regular training and education for employees, monitor compliance with regulations, and establish a system for reporting and addressing any issues or violations that arise. Compliance can be a complex and ongoing process, and many businesses choose to work with compliance professionals or consultants to help navigate the regulatory landscape.

7.2 Creating a Compliance Program

Creating a compliance program is essential for businesses to ensure they are following all applicable laws and regulations. A compliance program is a set of policies and procedures that a company implements to ensure it is in compliance with legal requirements and industry standards.

The first step in creating a compliance program is to conduct a risk assessment to identify areas where the company may be at risk for noncompliance. This assessment should consider the company's industry, size, and operations, as well as any past violations or enforcement actions. Once potential risks are identified, the company can develop policies and procedures to address them. This may include training programs for employees, establishing reporting procedures for potential violations, and implementing controls to ensure compliance.

It's also important for companies to regularly review and update their compliance program to ensure it remains effective and relevant. This may involve conducting periodic risk assessments, updating policies and procedures as needed, and monitoring the program's effectiveness through audits and other evaluations.

A robust compliance program is a key component of a company's risk management strategy and can help mitigate legal and financial risks associated with noncompliance.

7.3 Conducting Internal Audits and Investigations

Internal audits are conducted to assess the organization's compliance with applicable laws, regulations, policies, and procedures. The audit process involves reviewing documentation, interviewing employees, and observing processes to identify potential issues. The audit results provide valuable insights that can be used to develop and implement corrective actions.

Internal investigations, on the other hand, are conducted in response to suspected or actual non-compliance. These investigations may be triggered by employee reports, whistleblower complaints, or other indicators of non-compliance. The investigation process typically involves gathering evidence, conducting interviews, and documenting findings. The results of an investigation can help the organization take corrective action, identify the root cause of the issue, and prevent similar incidents from occurring in the future.

It is important for organizations to have established policies and procedures for conducting internal audits and investigations. These policies and procedures should include guidelines for reporting and escalating issues, preserving evidence, and protecting the confidentiality of those involved. It is also important to ensure that the individuals conducting the audits and investigations are trained and qualified to do so.

By conducting internal audits and investigations, organizations can proactively identify and address compliance issues before they become more serious problems. This can help protect the organization's reputation, mitigate legal and financial risks, and promote a culture of compliance within the organization.

7.4 Managing Business Risks

Businesses face a variety of risks, such as financial, operational, legal, and reputational risks. Managing these risks is an essential aspect of running a successful and sustainable business.

One way to manage risks is to identify them early on through risk assessments. A risk assessment involves identifying potential risks, analyzing the likelihood and potential impact of those risks, and developing strategies to mitigate or avoid them.

Another important aspect of managing business risks is having proper insurance coverage. Businesses should carefully consider the types of insurance they need, such as liability insurance, property insurance, and business interruption insurance.

It's also crucial for businesses to stay up-to-date on regulatory changes and compliance requirements that may affect their operations. Failing to comply with regulations can result in fines, legal disputes, and damage to the company's reputation. Therefore, businesses should regularly review their compliance programs and make necessary updates to ensure they are in line with current regulations.

Managing business risks involves being proactive, identifying potential risks, having proper insurance coverage, staying informed about regulatory changes, and maintaining an effective compliance program.

Chapter 8: Litigation and Dispute Resolution

Chapter 8 focuses on the legal procedures and strategies involved in resolving disputes between businesses or individuals, commonly referred to as litigation and dispute resolution. Disputes can arise for a variety of reasons, including breach of contract, torts, intellectual property infringement, and employment issues. In this chapter, we will explore the various stages of the litigation process, from filing a complaint to trial and post-trial motions. We will also discuss alternative dispute resolution methods, such as mediation and arbitration, as well as strategies for minimizing litigation risk and costs.

8.1 Understanding Litigation and Dispute Resolution

Litigation refers to the process of resolving disputes through the court system, while dispute resolution refers to the process of resolving disputes outside of the court system, such as through negotiation, mediation, or arbitration.

In this chapter, we will explore the various types of disputes that can arise in a business context, such as contract disputes, intellectual property disputes, and employment disputes. We will also discuss the advantages and disadvantages of litigation versus alternative dispute resolution methods, as well as the factors that should be considered when deciding which approach to take.

Understanding the litigation and dispute resolution process is crucial for any business owner or manager, as it can help them to avoid potential legal disputes and manage any disputes that do arise in a more effective and efficient manner.

8.2 Civil Litigation

Civil litigation is a legal process in which two or more parties seek to resolve a dispute or claim through the court system. In civil litigation, the plaintiff (the party bringing the claim) seeks damages or some other type of relief from the defendant (the party being sued).

Civil litigation can arise from a wide range of disputes, including contract disputes, employment disputes, intellectual property disputes, personal injury claims, and more. The process typically begins when the plaintiff files a complaint with the court, which sets out the claims and allegations against the defendant.

After the complaint is filed, the defendant has an opportunity to respond by filing an answer, which sets out the defendant's position and defenses to the claims. The parties then engage in a process called discovery, in which they exchange information and evidence relevant to the dispute.

After discovery is complete, the case may proceed to trial, where a judge or jury will hear evidence and arguments from both sides and make a decision. However, many civil disputes are settled before trial through negotiation or alternative dispute resolution methods, such as mediation or arbitration.

Civil litigation can be a lengthy and expensive process, so it is important for businesses to have a solid understanding of the potential risks and benefits before pursuing legal action.

8.3 Alternative Dispute Resolution Methods

Alternative Dispute Resolution (ADR) refers to methods of resolving disputes outside of traditional litigation in court. These methods are often more cost-effective, quicker, and less formal than litigation, and can help preserve relationships between parties.

The most common types of ADR are mediation and arbitration. Mediation involves a neutral third party (the mediator) facilitating a discussion between the parties in order to reach a mutually acceptable resolution.

The mediator does not make any decisions, but instead helps the parties communicate and negotiate. Arbitration, on the other hand, involves a neutral third party (the arbitrator) who hears arguments and evidence from both parties and then makes a binding decision. Arbitration can be either voluntary or mandatory, depending on the agreement between the parties.

Other types of ADR include negotiation, conciliation, and collaborative law. Negotiation involves the parties directly discussing and working out a resolution themselves. Conciliation is similar to mediation, but the third party (the conciliator) may take a more active role in suggesting solutions. Collaborative law involves each party hiring their own attorney and working together to reach a resolution, often with the help of other professionals such as financial advisors or therapists.

ADR can be a useful tool for businesses to manage and resolve disputes, particularly in cases where maintaining a positive business relationship is important. However, it is important to carefully consider the pros and cons of each method and consult with legal counsel before deciding on an approach to dispute resolution.

8.4 Enforcing Judgments and Awards

When a judgment or award is issued in favor of a party, it is important to ensure that it is enforced to its fullest extent. This may require additional legal action if the opposing party refuses to comply voluntarily.

Enforcement of judgments and awards may involve a number of legal procedures, including writs of execution, garnishments, and liens on property. It is important to work with an experienced attorney to navigate these complex legal processes and ensure that your rights are protected.

It is important to understand that even if a judgment or award is obtained, there may still be challenges in collecting the full amount owed. This can be especially true if the opposing party is financially insolvent or lacks the assets to satisfy the judgment or award.

It is important to have a solid understanding of the enforcement process and to work with an experienced attorney to protect your interests and rights in any litigation or dispute resolution process.

Chapter 9: International Business Law

Chapter 9: International Business Law explores the legal considerations and challenges that arise when conducting business across national borders. As the global marketplace continues to expand and businesses operate across multiple jurisdictions, it is crucial for entrepreneurs and businesses to understand the legal framework and regulations that govern international business transactions. This chapter covers various aspects of international business law, including international trade agreements, cross-border contracts, intellectual property protection, foreign investment laws, and dispute resolution mechanisms. With the knowledge and understanding gained from this chapter, businesses can effectively navigate the legal complexities of conducting business internationally and minimize their risk of legal disputes and financial losses.

9.1 International Business Law Overview

International business law involves the legal frameworks, regulations, and agreements that govern business transactions and relationships between entities from different countries. These laws are put in place to promote fair trade practices and prevent conflicts between businesses operating in different jurisdictions.

International business law is becoming increasingly important as globalization continues to expand and more businesses seek to expand their operations internationally. Companies need to be aware of the legal requirements and risks involved when conducting business across borders, including compliance with local laws, regulations, and trade agreements.

Some of the key areas of international business law include international trade agreements, cross-border investments, intellectual property protection, international dispute resolution, and compliance with foreign regulations. Understanding these legal frameworks and their implications for business operations is crucial for companies that engage in international trade and investment.

9.2 Cross-border Transactions

cross-border transactions refer to commercial activities between parties in different countries. Such transactions can take various forms, including import and export of goods, licensing and franchising agreements, joint ventures, and mergers and acquisitions.

International business laws govern cross-border transactions and vary from country to country. Companies engaging in cross-border transactions need to be aware of the legal requirements, regulations, and potential risks involved in conducting business abroad. These legal requirements include, but are not limited to, import/export regulations, tax laws, labor laws, intellectual property laws, and trade agreements.

When conducting cross-border transactions, companies need to comply with the laws and regulations of both their home country and the host country. They also need to understand the cultural differences, language barriers, and business practices of the host country to avoid misunderstandings and conflicts.

To ensure compliance with international business laws and regulations, companies may seek legal advice from international business lawyers or engage in international trade organizations, such as the World Trade Organization (WTO), to obtain information and guidance.

9.3 Export Controls and Compliance

export controls refer to regulations and laws that restrict and regulate the export of certain products, technologies, and information. These controls aim to ensure national security, prevent terrorism, and protect human rights. Companies that engage in international business must comply with export controls to avoid penalties, fines, and legal liability.

Export controls apply to various products, such as military goods and dual-use items, which have both civilian and military applications. They also apply to technology and software, technical data, and encryption products. Companies must conduct due diligence to determine if their products are subject to export controls and obtain the necessary licenses and permits before exporting them.

Export compliance programs help companies ensure compliance with export controls. These programs include policies and procedures for screening and classifying products, identifying end-users and end-uses, obtaining export licenses, and conducting due diligence on customers and business partners. Companies must also train employees on export compliance and monitor their compliance with export control regulations.

9.4 Global Business Considerations

One major consideration is cultural differences, including language barriers, social norms, and business customs. Companies must take the time to understand these differences to avoid misunderstandings and potential legal issues.

Another consideration is the political and economic stability of the countries where the company operates. Changes in government, laws, or financial systems can affect a company's ability to do business and may increase risks such as political unrest, expropriation, and currency fluctuations.

Intellectual property rights are also a significant concern for companies operating internationally. They must ensure that their trademarks, copyrights, and patents are adequately protected in each country where they do business, as laws and regulations vary from one country to another.

Furthermore, companies must comply with the various legal requirements and regulations of each country where they operate, including tax laws, labor laws, and environmental regulations. This can be challenging as regulations vary significantly between countries and regions.

Companies must have a thorough understanding of the legal systems and dispute resolution mechanisms available in each country where they do business. Different legal systems can have different requirements for contracts, intellectual property rights, and other legal matters. Additionally, companies must be aware of the various dispute resolution mechanisms available, including litigation, arbitration, and mediation.

Conclusion

In conclusion, understanding business law is an essential aspect of running a successful business. This book has covered a wide range of topics related to business law, including contracts, taxation, intellectual property, employment law, compliance, and international business law.

One of the key takeaways from this book is the importance of seeking legal advice early on in the business formation process. This can help entrepreneurs avoid costly mistakes and ensure that they are operating within the bounds of the law. It is also important for businesses to regularly review and update their legal documentation to ensure that they remain compliant with any changes in the law.

Another important aspect of business law is managing risk. Businesses must identify potential risks and take steps to mitigate them. This includes developing compliance programs and conducting internal audits and investigations. It also involves implementing effective dispute resolution methods, such as alternative dispute resolution, to avoid costly litigation.

Intellectual property is another crucial aspect of business law. Businesses must protect their intellectual property, including trademarks, patents, and copyrights, to maintain a competitive advantage in the market. This requires a thorough understanding of intellectual property laws and the ability to enforce them.

Employment law is another important area of business law. Employers must understand their legal obligations to their employees, including wage and hour laws, discrimination laws, and health and safety regulations. Failure to comply with these laws can result in costly lawsuits and damage to a company's reputation.

Taxation is yet another critical area of business law. Understanding tax laws and regulations is essential for businesses to remain compliant and avoid penalties. It is also important to work closely with tax professionals to identify potential tax deductions and ensure that businesses are taking advantage of all available tax breaks.

Finally, international business law is becoming increasingly important as businesses expand into new markets. Companies must understand the legal and regulatory frameworks of the countries they operate in and ensure compliance with international laws and regulations.

Understanding business law is crucial for businesses of all sizes and industries. It requires a thorough understanding of a wide range of legal topics, including contracts, intellectual property, employment law, taxation, compliance, and international business law. Businesses must take a proactive approach to managing legal risks and seek legal advice early on in the business formation process. By doing so, businesses can avoid costly mistakes and ensure that they remain compliant with all relevant laws and regulations.

www.ingramcontent.com/pod-product-compliance
Lightning Source LLC
Chambersburg PA
CBHW080622220526
45466CB00010B/3428